ERICA JETT

Be Good
TO YOU

"The Journey Of A Transformed Woman"

Be Good to You

Published by Lee's Press and Publishing Company
www.LeesPress.net

Lee's PRESS | *A Premiere Self-Publishing Services Company*

ISBN-13: 978-1-964234-09-0

PAPERBACK

TABLE OF CONTENTS

Dedication 1

Chapter 1: Identified as a Nobody 2

Chapter 2: The Face of Lost 8

Chapter 3: The Danger in Measurement 13

Chapter 4: The Balance of Life 18

Chapter 5: I Want My Portion 25

Chapter 6: The Power of Changing 33

Chapter 7: Being Woke Every Day 40

Chapter 8: The Spirit of a Champion 46

Polishing My Jewels Hidden in My Backyard3 49

Chapter 9: Rescue Her 53

Chapter 10: Being Good to Me Is My New Purpose 57

DEDICATION

I dedicate this book to my Lord and Savior; and to my husband Timothy Jett, who shows up daily to our lives.

To my favorite son, Dela Quick, who has been standing by my side.

To my grands, who gives me a greater reason to appreciate living and to my enemies, who made sure I completed the race, even though that wasn't their intention.

Chapter One

IDENTIFIED AS A NOBODY

A tribute to every woman who was labeled a nobody, even by themselves!

Have you ever heard those fatal words designed to break you or, even worse, destroy you? Some words can crush your spirit and kill your potential before it even can live! Words like: "You will never amount to anything, you don't have what it takes, you are fat, you are too skinny, you are not enough, you are dumb, you are stupid, you are a loser, you think you are better, and you are a *nobody*." After hearing words like these on a continuous basis, how could you be good to you, when your thoughts about yourself was derogatory?

What is a nobody? Have you researched the definition? "Nobody" is a person of no importance, a person who is not fashionable in society and has no authority. Also, a person with no influence!

Believing you are a nobody means agreeing you don't matter, that your *life* doesn't matter! This type of belief will cause you to continually ask yourself, "Why am I here? I don't see the importance of existing."

I dedicate this chapter to everyone who has been led into the wilderness of hopelessness about themselves!

Hopelessness is a dark place. It shouts and shuts us in walls of abandonment, closing in and claiming that recovery is beyond us!

If we never look inside and ask why our lives are not beating properly, never really investigate it, we will find we have been breathing in toxin!

Toxin is a deadly poison; it kills dreams and destinies! Toxin is a bad virus that begins to spread into every ounce of our lives, drying things up until they decay, and ultimately bringing destruction!

Stop right here and reread the first portion so you can begin the process of detangling from this web! Can you see what is really holding you back from living?

I dedicate this chapter to every woman who has been ashamed, who lives in the shadows of this voice! I am here to speak up and encourage you to rise above that lie that wants to crush your very existence!

What is true about the accusation that you are a nobody? The truth is *you* are a high commodity; you are someone that is highly valued. You are in much demand!

Your existence alone is a threat because it clearly speaks to your continued survival! You are an influencer with the power to bring an effect, whether directly or indirectly. Understand that you are shaped by God, and through Him, the scripture becomes true: you are fearfully and wonderfully made!

You have been tamed to live beneath the unloaded gun that has been daring you to come out. You fear what that unloaded gun can do. The perception of the gun permitted it to point at you; it made you stay hidden, kept you bound, made you timid, because you only see your limitations! The pointed gun has you only seeing your failures! The pointed gun has you only seeing the impossibilities; it makes you believe you are undone and incomplete!

But you forgot to realize this gun has no bullets; it's unloaded! Stop allowing the enemy and your self-abuse to hold the trigger, daring and threatening you! You have been given a sword and a shield!

Do you know how to use these protective weapons to make room for what is already yours? The Shield of Faith will block everything and thought that denies power over God's Word about what He says to you! When you believe in Jesus and accept Him, you can quench every fiery dart thrown at you. You will lift the shield and let it block for you! You will swing the Sword of the Spirit, the Word of God, and use their combined power. When every doubt, every trial, and every temptation begin to aggress what you believe, open your mouth and swing the Strength and Power of God by saying, "It is written!" This will let you bring His Word to pass.

It's decision time! You clearly now have insight. You must be willing to release your "nobody syndrome." It is time to take brave steps into the light and start the process of being good to you!

Choosing to *be good to you* is not normal to us, but it must become our new normal!

Being good to you is the proper birthing place where things can finally live at their greatest potential!

It's time to walk out of the shadows and the rules of a nobody and claim a new status! When we continue to live in dark places, that serves unfruitful places, and causes us to live beneath our potential. We suck on the pacifier of the lie that says, "You can't go any further," "Nobody has ever done it," or "Who do you think you are?" Come off the pacifier! You are not a baby anymore!

Respond! Be good to you! Speak your truth!

Why is this important? We do not wrestle against flesh and blood, but against the rulers, against the authorities, against the cosmic powers over this present darkness, against the spiritual forces of evil in the heavenly places. As you can see, we live in a world that operates in darkness.

Darkness is more than the absence of light or the opposite of light! Darkness is something that occupies space and has dimension. Darkness has a negative tone that forbids entrance into a place from which there is no escape. The place it covers, as we learned, is a place that crushes, presses down, and destroys those who enter its perilous domain. Darkness is a place one should ever desire to enter.

John 8:12

*Then spake Jesus again unto them, saying, "I am the **light** of the world: he that follow me shall not walk in darkness, but shall have the **light** of life."*

Say out loud:

This is the season that I will be *good to me*!

I will not allow venomous thoughts into my life!

I will begin to sum up my life. I will do my best by filling my mind with and meditating on things that are true, noble, reputable, authentic, compelling, and gracious. I will focus on the best, not the worst; the beautiful, not the ugly; things to praise, not things to curse!

Being good to you is not a selfish act but one God designed to bring forth abundance!

Being good to you is not a superficial act. Instead, it is the art of living the *qualified life!*

Living in that light takes us to the most freeing and growing fruitful place anyone should want to walk! It is the *most beautiful* place!

To be good to you, you must first enter the God Zone!

Inside the God Zone is where everything begins to flow because of our willingness to accept, believe, and receive the plan of Jesus, His only Son!

John 3:16

For God so loved the world, that He gave His only Son, that whosoever believe in Him should not perish, but have everlasting life.

Being good to you demands a life showered with balance and wholeness.

Do you have a healthy stream of water abounding in you? Is your inner stream of water mixed with brokenness, stress, disappointment, uncertainty, lack of wisdom, lack of confidence, irresponsibility? A healthy inner means having God in the center of our lives. Having a trust in God that makes ashes turn to beauty, you will have the oil of gladness instead of mourning, and a mantle of praise instead of a spirit of fainting.

Step into the light and realize there is better on your side than against you! I know we would all love to reset the clock and start some things over, but wishing to go back is harmful to us! We must release the past; we must understand we can't change it. We must be better people, must learn and grow so our present *and* our future are brighter!

A fresh start is now on the schedule of your life! Do you walk away, or do you check in and do the work God is asking of you?

There are three things you must continue to keep you in the God Zone so you can start *being good to you*!

1. Acknowledge God. A grateful heart sends out a pure sound! He is worthy! A great practice is committing a month to reading all of the Psalms in the Bible.

2. Acknowledge who you are. Your identity is now in Christ, not in anything else. Study who He says you are and live from that place!

3. Renew your mind. Choosing wisely to sit and learn to grow so good fruit will be on display in your life! Be good to God and, in return, He will teach you to *be good to you*!

Chapter 2

THE FACE OF LOST

A tribute to every woman who has ever been lost!

Losing does not mean failure. Instead, it is a place we could not find or retain.

What have you lost in your life? The list is very long; I get it! We have all experienced the highs and lows of being lost! We have lost so much; we are camped out in a hole. Let us deal with that hole where we go sit and recount how far behind, we are in our lives! We can then begin to feed ourselves what we consider our reality!

The older woman says, "It's too late to get married. Besides, who wants a woman at my age?"

The single woman says, "There are no good men out there. They are all dogs!"

The struggling woman says, "I will never own my own house or leave this abusive relationship!"

The unhappy married woman says, "I will never change. My finances will never get better!"

The woman with degrees says, "I am stuck in this nine-to-five job."

These statements make these women feel they are losing, that they live in the realm of impossibilities! These words are equations for the losing syndrome; they continue as you sit in that hole until you say a lost person's famous last words: "It is *never* going to happen!" Never is such a strong word and it means at no time, in the past or future; on no occasion; not

8

ever, not at all, will you ever arrive at a good place or release your greatest potential! Losing is an equation, and an equation is meant to be solved!

You may ask, "Why do I stay in the losing realm? Why does it seem like I cannot get out?" One reason is because of life in itself! Life is an unexpected journey with unexpected curves that either make or break us!

Life is the embodiment of selfishness! Life is selfish because it is for itself in two ways: it is for its own survival, and it is for its own reproduction!

Life is filled with uncertainty and people with different cultures, languages, and behavioral patterns! You see individuals trying to march to a certain beat, which can sometimes create barriers and make life more complicated! When things are different from us and our ways of doing things, we might not mix but collide. Nothing but chaos will come from collision! We are influencers, but we can't control people or change them into copies of ourselves. We need to stop wanting to see people become us. Instead, we need to develop and inspire radical change within ourselves. Only then will we begin to see other things come into alignment. Be good to you and start eliminating these barriers of misconception that interrupt your flow and vibes.

"People will be people" is a common saying, but I want you to add to this statement that "God is God." What does that mean, "God is God"? He changes not because He does not have to. Why is that? Because he lacks nothing. But our lives need substance, clarity, conciseness, stability, and surety! We need the confidence of God and His wisdom to guide us. He will release all doubts clouding our lives.

I realized, at one time in my life, I not only lived in the shadows but hid because of so many false realities. I have been hurt, abused, disappointed, let down; I did not how to become unstuck. So, I stayed stuck! Being in a stuck place was not my intention.

I wanted to be better. I wanted my life to be better. But I had already counted myself out of the game of life. I literally hated myself. I would stand in the mirror and call myself the names others would call me. I said so many harmful words to myself. I was hostile. I would even slap myself until I finally broke down in tears.

My spirit was crushed and bleeding. I did not know how to be good to me because I did not know what that looked like. If you hate anything about you, I beg you now to reconsider. Challenge yourself to see yourself in God's light. I had to reverse this curse over my life, renew my mind, and act. I stood in front of that mirror as I would say not just positive things about my life, but the truth.

Do you see the difference? Truth is a seed that breaks me free from every lie. Speaking God's truth was hard because I was out of my comfort zone. I was changing how I always viewed myself. I could not even look myself in the eye. Every time I would smile, I would cover my mouth. I pray you seek God and talk to a believer to encourage you out of your madness. The best way to find a better space in your life is by being truthful where you are. Then, allow God entrance, and believe you are worthy of becoming.

Having a lack of confidence is not our fault. But once it is brought to our attention, it is our fault when we don't address it. It is important to know the factors that contribute to low self-confidence, for they often involve a combination of things and are different for everyone. Your genetics, cultural background, childhood experiences, and other life circumstances all play a role. But don't lose heart. Although we can't change the past experiences that shaped us, there is plenty we can do to alter our thoughts and expectations to gain more confidence.

We can no longer allow our pasts to keep us stuck in this cycle. We must get past how people view us and let go of our trauma. We need to heal and gain confidence because we will not be able to live in joy and we will never be impactful.

Two things helped me increase my confidence. One day, I had to minister to a group of ladies I saw as better than me. I was so nervous, and I wasn't used to speaking to groups. So, one of my friends called to pray with me before I went to speak. My friend said, "Erica, don't have confidence in yourself. Have confidence in God!" I immediately felt the pressure release. My friend continued, "You have God in you. Besides, it's His people and His word." I still, to this day, follow that truth. It helps me overcome my fear of speaking or moving forward in my life.

Another time, I was sharing with someone my feelings of inadequacy, how my mistakes felt like they were hanging over me. The individual said, "Erica, stop beating yourself up. It does not define you." Confidence says to own your weakness, but do not let them define your self-worth. You are more than your degrees, your popularity, the amount of money you make. God, forbid you lose any of those things and lose yourself in the process. I have seen it happen.

Instead, let us be clear-minded and accept the realities of things. Let us grow in God, in character, and Godly wisdom. Let me tell you, these practices will give you the best confidence you can achieve. It is time to be good to you! We will stop making excuses for why we can't move forward. We make no space for negativity to continue to rule our lives. Today, we allow ourselves room to grow, expand, and live this life unafraid. And we show up to our lives every day being good to us. Everything else will flow from that place.

Chapter 3

THE DANGER IN MEASUREMENT

A tribute to women who have dealt with seeing everyone's beauty but their own!

I used to hate mirrors because I viewed them as critical tools that only reflected my flaws. But I know some people who hate and love the mirror. Today I like having a mirror because I know how to properly use it.

We need to take a moment to examine our beauty and our lanes in life. If we continue to measure ourselves to others, we will stifle our growth. We will never have arrived at our destination because we'll have been traveling in others' lanes, having more excitement for their lives than our own. I am guilty; I have seen places and people I'd rather be. You begin to see all that beauty and ask yourself why you aren't as good-looking, why you don't have a husband, don't live in a new house, don't have the newest clothes, why you can't have children. Immediately, our calculations are off because we are counting others' blessings and not our own. We are truly blind not to see our blessings; it really shows where we are in our character. As we journey through being good to ourselves, we must know we are enough!

When we measure ourselves against one another, we begin to compare. Comparison breeds feelings of envy, low self-confidence, and depression. These emotions compromise our ability to trust others and see ourselves as gifts. When we compare, we devalue ourselves. That is dangerous territory.

We must be clear that we can be anything, but we can't be everything. When we compare ourselves to others, we're often comparing their best features to our average ones. For example, someone who is a good speaker may want to sing professionally, but that's not their gift. So, they compare themselves to others, convincing themselves of their inability, not realizing they are being self-destructive. Comparison between two people is a recipe for unhappiness. There is one thing you're better at than other people: being you. This is where you really shine: being you and developing you.

When you understand your beauty, you can stop comparing yourself and begin to see how our differences play a major part in making one great, beautiful sound on Earth. We all complement one another. Truly, that is what we miss in this day and age. The beauty mark not every individual and working together to achieve something greater than all of us. Life becomes about being a better version of yourself. And when that happens, your effort and energy go toward upgrading your personal operating system every day, not worrying about what others are doing.

You are enough to begin to be registered in the deepest part of our being. When you own your lane, your beauty, your gifts, you break free from the shackles of false comparisons and focus on the present moment. We also measure ourselves to others when we give all we have, produce our best work, and don't receive the praise we expect. Listen, when what you do doesn't meet the criteria, or expectations, of others—too bad. What really matters is what you think about what you do, what your standards are, that you do your best. That's not an excuse to ignore thoughtful opinions, other people might give you a picture of how you fall short of being your best self. Be open to positive criticism; it will make you grow.

When you stop comparing yourself to others and focus internally, you become better at what really matters: being you. It's simple but not easy. Compare yourself to who you were yesterday—now that is a *real* comparison—and that will bring forth fruit.

Another thing we must embrace so we can begin to stop comparing ourselves is defining our beauty. Defining your beauty, and expanding your definition of *beautiful*, will inspire you to find peace, comfort, and joy in your own skin. We must take the time to discover, define, and ultimately love the qualities that make each of us unique. There are some things only you can do. Knowing your true beauty helps you come alive and shape the realities of vulnerability and adversity. That knowledge will help you create a brave space for deep personal reflection, enabling you to uncover unique aspects of your identity. As you grow in your beauty, you will learn to harness the power of your uniqueness and gain the confidence to share your beauty. Growing creates opportunities for you to reach your full potential and define your beauty.

A transition must happen so you can abandon ingrained fears and biases from old programming. When you are in transition, you are willing to go through the process of changing from one state or condition to another. When you refuse to change or break down hindering barriers, you lose the ability to properly see yourself. This transition is important; it helps you see God and yourself. When you deal with feelings of loss, feel disconnected from life, you might hold on to ingrained fears and negative biases based on old programming. We fear failure, so we measure, we self-sabotage, and use that as an excuse to not move forward.

You need to shift your perspective and attitude. Realize failure is only discovery; it shows us what doesn't work. It's an opportunity to try again with more intelligence. So, don't be afraid to fail. It doesn't matter what happened when you were growing up or how many times you failed in the past; get up and try again. The past doesn't have to hinder your future. Start doing your best and let bygones be bygones. Live in the present, learn from the past, and chart the way toward the desired life—the life designed for you by God. To seek His plan—it is going to be worth it in the end.

I used to wake up every day to the mental reminder of each of my failures, wishing I could have another chance at life. God spoke to me and commanded me to stop bringing my yesterday into today. I was mistreating my new days. I began to recite the Serenity Prayer.

God, grant me the serenity to accept the things I cannot change, the courage to change the things I can, and the wisdom to know the difference.

Each day is special and important to achieving our vision, plan, and purpose. We must wake up and execute—not sleep in and only wish, but pray, plan, and press.

It is time to take ownership of your life and live above the line. Are you living above the line or below the line? Are there some concepts you see, hear, and agree with, but don't take the time to really digest the depth of them? What is living above the line? It is not allowing anything to live above the authority of God's truth. You must recognize you have the power to change the results of your life. Yes, sometimes this is easier said than done (especially when you've had a challenging past).

Living below the line essentially means giving your power away to other people and external situations. A fish is successful underwater because that environment suits their progression. Our environment is on land, but we want to hang out underwater and only come for breaths. But that is not living, that is surviving. We are made for more, and that is how we must begin to live—on land and unafraid. We must not measure ourselves against others or our failures. Be willing to rise and live above the line.

To live above the line, you must be willing to blame others for situations, making excuses, living in denial, and having a sense of entitlement. You must take personal responsibility. You cannot change the circumstances, the seasons, or the wind, but you can change yourself with the guidance of the Spirit of God. George Washington Carver said, "Ninety-nine percent of all failures come from people who have a habit of making excuses." You will be that one percent living above the line.

Chapter 4

THE BALANCE OF LIFE

*A tribute to all women who want to reach a higher
standard in every area of their life!*

There is a formula to everything; without the formula, it
will not work. A formula is a standard or accepted way of doing
or making something real. Understand there is no magic formula
to achieve the greatness of your life. But there is a set of standards
or guidelines to better your life long-term.

God is the first formula we need to follow. God is not
optional in our lives; he is the *necessity*, the glue that brings
everything together. Jesus is the cornerstones in the temples;
without the stones that hold up every corner of our lives, we
will fail miserably.

Ephesians 2:19-22

*Now therefore, you are no longer strangers and foreigners,
but fellow citizens with the saints and members of the
household of God, having been built on the foundation of
the apostles and prophets, Jesus Christ Himself being the
Chief Cornerstone, in who the whole building, being fitted
together, grows into the temple in the Lord, in who you also
are being built together for a dwelling place of God in the
Spirit.*

We can't think our greatest achievement is to own stuff
and lack substance. Stuff is an accumulation of things that
limit our capacity for growth. Substance is the maturity of
the right portions to manifest the totality of everything about
us. Substance is the ultimate reality that underlies all outward

manifestations and change. You have heard the famous quote that a mind is a terrible thing to waste, but a wonderful thing to invest in.

It's difficult for a finite mind to comprehend an infinite God; it is like trying to put an ocean in a glass. However, that doesn't mean we shouldn't try. We lack the ability to let go of certain things in our lives because we lack knowledge of our God and His abilities. We must understand that the whole of creation flows from the substance of God. The Christ story is the universe story. The birth of the divine-human child is a revelation, a lifting of the veil to show us that all life has been conceived by the Spirit in the womb of the universe. We are all divine human creatures; everything alive in the universe carries within itself the sacredness of the Spirit. We must tap into God to reach our greatest potential.

We must focus on who God is, who we are in Him. When we reflect God's image in our life, when we look through his lens, every aspect of our life will be promoted. We are ready for real growth.

To disobey the formula of God's Word would be a direct attack on the eternity and your position. Let us take a closer look at disobedience! Disobedience is a defiance of authority and a failure or refusal to obey rules and orders.

I remember a time I was putting together a bookshelf and refused to follow the instructions. I had decided to do it my own way, and once I had the bookshelf up, it looked good, even though I'd left out major pieces. When I stepped back, I saw it was leaning and unstable. I tried to convince myself it didn't look that bad. But that was an excuse. I did not want to redo it because it would take too much time, and I did not have the patience. I just wanted the bookshelf to hold my books, so I decided to deal with the lean of the shelf no matter how it looked.

I disobeyed the bookshelf's instructions and ignored its intended layout. This is what we do with our lives and why we lack balance when we don't follow precise rules or guidelines. We omit things to fit our comfort levels, then wonder why we don't see the manifestation of things. Once again, we are using stuff when we need substance. We have to follow the formula in every part of our lives to see change.

What is the remedy for disobedience? It is simple; be obedient! Being obedient is the total surrender to an order without considering whether you agree. How many excuses do people give to justify their inaccurate perceptions? We must not conform; we must transform to see our lives balanced.

We often change our attitudes and behaviors to match the attitudes and behaviors of the people around us. One reason for this conformity is a concern about what other people think of us. We'd rather blend in and compromise what we know to be true. We often conform to the norm because others have information we do not. In this way, relying on norms can be a reasonable strategy, especially when we're uncertain about how we should act. People rarely care about how you feel about the issue at hand; they just want you to agree with them. But being balanced involves having the courage to live in absolute truth, no matter what the unpopular opinion is.

Proverbs 3: 1-2

My son [or daughter], do not forget my law, but let my heart keep my commands; for length of day and long life and peace they will add to you.

There is a great reward for those who obey and a warning for those who do not take heed. What is the reward God promised to the man or woman who will keep His commandments? Long life! Obedience can affect one's length of days. As a general principle, if we seek to live in the will of God and obey His laws, our days will be lengthened. But if we break His laws by living careless, intemperate, self-led lives, our days may be shortened. Protection is an incentive for obedience. There is a wonderful promise in the following verse.

Ecclesiastes 8:5

Whoever keeps a command will know no evil thing and the wise heart knows the right time and procedure.

This does not mean nothing will go wrong if we obey God. It means we should know that, in all things, God works for the good of those who love Him, who have been called according to His purpose (Romans 8.28). We may experience sorrow, trials, and tests, but as they come through Him, they will never be evil, and always work out for our good.

Gladness is a fruit of the spirit; it is the most joyful thing in the world where people who are constantly seeking to keep God's commandments and please Him. Obey God, and you will discover the secret of abiding joy.

There is also great peace for those who keep God's commandments. Those who love God's instructions do not stumble. What a priceless reward this is—to enjoy great peace even in this world of trouble, fear, and war.

We partake in the assurance of salvation when we are obedient. Many Christians lack the assurance of their salvation, but God wants us to know we are eternally secure in Christ. Keeping His commandments, you will not only know but experience His divine plan for you. When we comply, we will receive answers to all our prayers. There is also a wonderful promise where we discover why our prayers are not answered. If we seek to obey God, He promises to answer our prayers. What a reward!

The conscious presence of Christ ensures us that the Lord is always with us. We are only made conscious of His presence when we are obeying Him. What does it mean to keep God's commandments? It means seeking Him and adhering to the system of God. We cannot know the commandments until we find them, and we can only find them by seeking and being obedient to them. This seeking is a life-long occupation; obeying them promptly and delighting in obeying God brings a reward.

When you are supposed to be working—work. And when you are supposed to be playing—play. It is a strange tightrope you are walking, but it's only when you get your priorities mixed up that things fall apart. People always ask, what does a balanced life really mean? What would a balanced life look like to us? And most importantly, how do we go about achieving that middle ground amidst our crazy schedules? There are steps you can take to change what is not working and reclaim some control and balance in your life. And once you start seeing results, you will be better equipped to maintain that new equilibrium. The key is not to try to change everything at once, but to make small adjustments over time to determine what works for you. Eventually, you will have a whole new set of positive life habits; you'll never look back!

There are certain ways you can achieve balance in your daily life that will help you be more productive. Learn to turn it off; make room for things that will add value instead of things that fill your days with excess. I remember when I did not look at television for forty days straight because I had grown to use it as a distraction. When I turned it off, my focus went to things that improved my life. I became stronger and overall different. What do you need to turn off to make room for the right things to bring fulfillment to your life?

Sometimes we must trim, to remove some things because of excess. I remember when I wanted to take my relationship with God to the next level, but I was still clubbing. My girl buddy and I would dress up and go to parties. Inside my mind, I heard God requesting my presence. His voice was strong; I had to remove clubbing from my life. I was changing; wherever God led me, I had to adjust. You have to say no to anything either nonessential or superfluous to your life.

Be ruthless! You must pay attention to your health! People are dying in daily life because they neglect their health. The bad part is we know what we need to do, and what it takes, we just don't take action. Our health needs to become a priority; do not let us wait for a health emergency. Our health affects the quality of our lives and our work. We are far more productive and at peace when we get enough sleep, eat a little healthier, and engage in some type of activity.

Good health also means minimizing toxins and removing negative influences. We must avoid toxic people (complainers, whiners, poor attitudes). If you're unable to completely avoid them, at least minimize contact, and tune them out as much as you can. Surround yourself with positive, supportive, can-do people whenever possible.

We must also prioritize spending time alone. We are people who are overworked and overwhelmed; alone time is crucial for lowering stress, increasing joy, and encouraging creativity. Learn to treat yourself! Sometimes we do so much for others that we aren't good to ourselves.

We must stay plugged into relationships. Set aside quality time with your family and friends. Plan lunch dates, family game nights, or simply call and pray with your friends. The one thing I am learning to help me stay balanced is to expand my awareness. I like taking a class or watching *Animal Kingdom* on the Discovery Channel. I like visiting new places, trying new things, and remembering to have fun. You don't need to go through this life being like a yo-yo, up and down. You do not have to feel like your life is out of control. Begin to take appropriate action and turn your life around now. Chances are, you will live the same routine for the rest of your time. Maybe life is uncertain for you right now, but you are capable of reclaiming control. Live a life well-balanced, not excessively, and you will live in harmony.

Chapter 5

I WANT MY PORTION

A tribute to any woman who wants her portion in life!

When you finally stop thinking about what everybody wants for you, you can begin asking yourself the most challenging yet rewarding question: "What do I want?" We cannot be afraid to expect good things. "Why not dream, Erica?" is a question I would often ask myself. As I got older, I realized I was the only thing in the way of achieving my life dreams. We all want to change our lives, but many of us aren't sure what we want our lives to be. Knowing what you want is the first and most important step in creating a better future. But how do you make this important decision? Trying to decide what you want in a world with so many decisions and choices can seem overwhelming.

Most of us have a really good idea of what we *don't* want in life. We take a glance at our lives and think about the things that do not feel right, such as an unsupportive spouse, kids who do not listen, or an empty checking account. You may have thoughts like, "I don't want to be poor," "I don't want to work for someone else forever," or "I don't want to be overweight all my life." The good news is, if you can identify what you don't want, knowing what you do want is within your grasp.

To perceive anything, there must be a contrast between the two states. To know something is unwanted, we must know something else is wanted instead. You can identify what you don't want because you know some other preferable state exists. Otherwise, you would not know it is unwanted. We must give more of our attention to the wanted state and give it some clarity. Once you have identified what you do not want, see if you can flip it over and consider the contrasting wanted state.

You may desire not to remarry because you got hurt and are afraid of being vulnerable again. On the other hand, if you have a desire to remarry, decide what will not work but be open to love. You might say, "I don't like to walk on a treadmill to lose weight, but I will begin to walk outside and choose a plan that is right for me to see the pounds drop." We must get as specific as possible! The more details you include, the more you can develop your plan and the steps necessary to achieve your goal.

Deciding what you want today does not mean you cannot change your mind tomorrow. Often, we think we want something, but as we find out more about it, we change our minds. Consider this a success, not a failure. Sometimes you realize either it was not good for you, or it might not be the right time. Keep in mind that there is a destination in life. Every time you obtain something you want; you have a new perspective from which you see other possibilities. Choosing something you want does not mean giving up all other possibilities. It means opening the door to possibilities you did not know existed.

If you find yourself looking at your list of wants and doubting whether you can have those things, you may have an issue with your expectations for the future. You act on what you expect, not what you want—so your expectations need to align with your wants, or you will not be able to achieve them. To work on changing your expectations, you may wish to become intentional about what you include in your life—from possessions to relationships. It is quite okay to expect and anticipate things, but make room for life, and keep your faith. Even if it does not happen the way you think it should. Be good to you and realize the importance of your journey. Let nothing stop you as you move forward, no matter if the expectations worked in your favor or not. Have expectations but be their driver; don't let them drive you. If you give them control, you will find yourself broken down and depressed when those expectations falter. Give yourself wiggle room and practice the fruit of the Spirit as you move forward in claiming what is rightfully yours. Beware of setting unrealistic goals; they do not convey the truth of a challenging situation, nor the difficulties involved in something you want to achieve.

Let's ask ourselves what we want to accomplish in the next three months. Write it down. So, what if it's bigger than you? If you don't move with what you have, you will never reach the portion that is rightfully yours. What is your portion? You cannot be terrified of what might happen if you allow yourself to go there. Will everything fall apart or into place?

When you realize there is nothing behind you, you become a woman on track. You realize there is no point in going back, it would be nonsense, and it would be more painful than the unknown before you, no matter what that might be. You will not be able to go back! How you see yourself will fundamentally change. That is why, this time, you will succeed! After you begin to take the leap and pursue your portion, your purpose, you will begin to see it everywhere. Dan Sullivan once said, "Your eyes only see, and your ears only hear what your brain is looking for." Once you commit to living your dreams, the lids blinding your eyes will be lifted. You will start to see a completely new

27

world. You will notice opportunities that have been in your reach all along, ones your conscious mind simply did not see. The fundamental change taking place is your self-identity. This is the point of no return. Once this shift has happened, your world changes. Nothing is impossible for you. Your only limitation is your consciousness, which is quickly expanding. Whatever you want quickly becomes yours because you see what most people do not! When you can see it everywhere, you are sprinting. After you have crossed the threshold of decision, you will find a new wellspring of energy and passion.

You will no longer need willpower. Willpower is overrated; it is for amateurs. It's for people still conflicted about what to do. Once you've moved beyond *will* to *why*, you no longer must coax yourself into action. The decision has been made. In third grade, I said I was going to be an author. In my mind, I was always an author, but I never acted or took the proper steps to make that come to fruition. But today you are holding more than my first book; you are holding my dream in your hands. I did the work and made it possible. When you are willing to travel down the road of the unknown, you will thirst for knowledge, wisdom, and understanding. You will become both student and teacher to yourself. You will become a sponge, soaking up everything you can, creating loads of neural connections and schematic networks. You will learn the difference between logic and rules; you will have limitless freedom to break the rules and create new ones.

I love what God says: with men it is impossible, but with God all things are possible. When you begin to tap into your portion, thriving becomes your new language. Mediocrity does not own you anymore. You will be constantly applying new information to accelerate your progress. When something doesn't work, you don't stay there. Instead, you cut your losses and move on, detached from the need to be right. Instead, you want progress—you understand and serve. Humility is your banner!

Every day is a step closer to your ideal than the last. The future is only getting better and better. You are in creation mode. You are no longer chasing happiness or success. You are after something more potent. You have finally learned to embrace who you are, so you are not trying to compete with some external indicator of success. You know success is inevitable because you are in alignment. You can have your portion in life if you give up what you hate and what holds you back. Until one is committed, there is hesitancy, the chance to draw back, and always ineffectiveness. Concerning all acts of initiative (and creation), the moment one commits oneself, then providence moves too. All sorts of things happen to help one that would not otherwise have occurred.

Whatever you can do to achieve whatever dream you have—begin it. Boldness has genius and power in it. Begin it now! When you align with your destiny, things will change for you financially, intellectually, spiritually, and relationally. The right people will come into your life. You will have enough time and money to get moving. The right books, articles, and audio will find their way into your life at just the right time. You will become the vector for everything you need to accomplish your task. Do not question why—just gracefully, humbly, and gratefully receive.

The shocking truth is that receiving, at a conscious and evolved level, is your purpose. Have you ever heard the saying,

"When the student is ready, the teacher will appear"? When you are on a dedicated mission, others will help you make it real. You will have mentors who will teach you and radically accelerate your progress. Fans and supporters. Students who want to learn, and haters who are just as necessary as the others who enter your life. Your relationships are by far the most important aspect of your journey. You will begin attracting the right people in your life when you start doing the work. It begins with initiative and openness. Once you are ready to learn, you will have teachers. Higher up the mountain, your work will attract the very people who will help spread your message and forward your cause.

Living your dreams is not a cheap experience. It is supposed to require some effort, something from the depths of your soul. So even when you are tempted to quit, you will dig deep. And if for some reason you decide to quit, that will haunt you until you rectify that decision. As Oliver Wendell Holmes Jr. said, 'A mind that is etched by a new experience can never go back to its old dimensions.' You can never go back to the way things once were, even if for a time you pretend to. No matter how devastating your doubts, you will eventually regain the hope you once had. But now it will only be stronger and solidified.

You are no longer rigid in your thinking. You are open and inspired to take action, even if, in the moment, it feels extremely uncomfortable. You no longer operate on impulse. You are inclined to do things yourself that others might be uncomfortable with. You are completely open, ready, and moving. You no longer stall or wonder when you'll get a prompt. You respond immediately and automatically. And when you act on these impressions, you never regret it. You only regret when you do not act and are left to wonder what might have been.

The more open you become, the more you find yourself in places you never thought you would be. But do not question why you keep going, connecting the dots. Eleanor Roosevelt once said, "Great minds discuss ideas; average minds discuss events; small minds discuss people." Beyond the point of no return is freedom—freedom from triviality and mediocrity. No longer will you be able to engage in gossip or other destructive activities. These things won't make sense to you anymore. Your entertainment will become learning, growth, and deep connection instead of shallow and grand adventures.

Since you no longer limit what you can have in life, you regularly travel. You meet new and interesting people. Even the small become significant. You learn to be fully entertained by a few moments of isolated thought. British philosophical writer James Allen wrote, in his book *As a Man Thinketh*, "When a man makes his thoughts pure, he no longer desires impure food." When one area of your life is out of alignment, every other area of your life suffers. And you are increasingly aware when your top priorities are being neglected. You protect the essentials.

Furthermore, when you improve one area of your life, you grow in all areas—you are the system. Consequently, every small and incremental victory you experience creates a surge of momentum toward your ultimate ideal. When you start taking your dreams seriously, you will not initially be qualified. But as you take on greater responsibility, you will become qualified to do what you need to do. You will grow into your responsibilities and have increased power and influence. Taking on the right forms of responsibility can put life in easy mode. It's like injecting yourself with motivation steroids, producing urgency and desperation.

When you are desperate to walk in your purpose and your portion, you have more responsibility. You stop caring about what is just and fair. You aim to bring joy wherever you are and in whatever you are doing. You no longer live by conventional rules or wisdom. You are directed by the highest power in existence that is God and your awareness. Stay connected to God. When you do this, you will not just have your portion, but you will begin to subdue, multiply, and be fruitful, causing you to totally dominate.

When you are moving like this, you have decided to be good to yourself and live for more than sleep but purpose. As an evolved person, you are connected to God, who is not just the higher source but *the* source. You have learned to listen well. You have the obedience that gives you strength and the boldness to enter unknown territory. There, you will begin to see your life unfold. We only know in part, but as we trust God and move forward, He reveals His plan, His purpose, and that is how we get our portion.

Chapter 6

THE POWER OF CHANGING

A tribute to the women who dealt with crossroads in their lives and decided to move toward wisdom, understanding, and stronger boundaries!

I will never forget when I was in the darkest place of my life. I knew it was all over for me. I was blaming everything that happened to me; I lived by the emotions that created a negative realm in my life. If I had to describe my life, it was chaotic. My life was complete confusion and disorder. Patterns were leading me into dark holes, and I could not see my way out. Many people can be so critical of those living in darkness. But I did not need a critical voice. I needed a voice full of love, that would give me light and insight so I could move forward.

I was hurting, I was bleeding, and even when I wanted better for myself, I would make a mess because I *was* a mess. My life was on a merry-go-round, and I was spinning out of control, walking dizzy into doors that led me into depression. I would literally hit myself; yes, you heard me right. I would slap myself in the face, telling myself how dumb I was. I would punch myself in the legs and arms, feeling unworthy of anything good happening in my life. I would always think, if I were to die, maybe then, someone would notice and miss me. I would think, if I were to hit a tree head-on, remove my life from this world. This was my perfect solution to my chaotic situation. But in fact, it was selfish of me to end my life when I did not create it.

I did not realize how much baggage I carried; I was weighed down by life's heavy burdens. I was tired. I was at a crossroads in my life. So much stood in my way, but the main thing standing in my way was me. I always wanted change; I understood now that *I* needed to change. The day I decided and said, "I am ready for a new life," I realized I needed my mind to be renewed. My attitude and behavior needed major alignment. I was ready to jump in and begin the process of the new me.

I was not sure how I was going to release those years of self-hatred that continued to run my life. I was afraid, but I knew it was time to leave the chaos behind and really tap into the life that was all mine. The first thing I needed to do was surrender to my current status and to the possibilities of what could be. It takes courage to allow strong uncomfortable feelings. It's difficult to accept disappointment, anger, loneliness, brokenness, and grief instead of trying to force them away. But acceptance brings relief.

I began to tell myself, "Start with every small step and every small decision that will begin to bring you out." My life needed order: I needed to shift my habits. I wanted access to my life, but the mental shape I was in, I was not going to get it. I surrendered to God because I needed truth. I lived a lie for so many years; I needed to taste freedom in my life. I needed freedom because it is a system God created for us to live our optimal lives. Having an active process in my life, having truth, created boundaries I so desperately needed. Truth prepared me to handle pressure and the unexpected waves that do not ask before they take. Freedom began to speak of God's ability in me and helped me become grounded in every area and circumstance.

If we are ever going to see a different major result in our lives, we must cross over. The beauty of crossing over is that you can reach the escape route you need while slamming the door on old habits and cycles. When you cross over and stay focused on your tasks, a shift happens. We lose the tunnel vision on things that distract us from our growth and direction. Be good to you and stay focused. Do not give up on your journey. Keep reminding yourself why you do what you do.

Journaling should be a habit to help make your transition a greater experience. When you log for about ten minutes a day, you will begin to see a shift in your mindset and desires. Have a routine for your life to produce fruit in the areas in which you are seeking change. Prayer and the Word should be at the top of our lists to center where we are going. Set aside time to create monthly to-do lists. Be specific about where you are going and how you are going to get there. These routines will spark a desire to live in a positive space that will help you achieve your dreams. You will see your life reflect your destiny.

Life can be so demanding, and, yes, it causes uncertainty. Do become normalized, have structure and order, but embrace uncertainties. When uncertainty hits our lives, it sometimes makes us stretch in places we normally would not. Allow this to happen. Grow within the differences, the struggle. I live for boundaries because they mark the areas in my life I should not cross; they prevent other things from crossing into my spaces. Boundaries help us take control of our lives. I needed boundaries, and I needed to respect the boundaries I had in place because they were beneficial. My life could use some good news, some structure, some rewards when I get it right.

Healthy boundaries can serve to establish one's identity. Specifically, healthy boundaries can produce divine individuality and help people recognize what they will and will not hold themselves responsible for. Healthy boundaries are a crucial component of self-care. Poor boundaries lead to resentment, anger, burnout, and stress. Place boundaries wherever you need growth. Be ready to walk away from anything or anyone causing setbacks in your life. Walk away with an unshakable and rooted confidence to replace doubts in yourself. May we have the boldness to explore and face the fears that are stopping us.

We need strength to stand in places we never stood in before. Strength helps us break free from old patterns. Trust your judgment, even if you may be wrong. Stay open; nobody knows everything. Trust your abilities. Finally, dare to act and explore how different your life could be. There is a lie that you no longer have to feel exhausted or frustrated. In this new life, in your transformation, you will eliminate the pain of underperformance and stop second-guessing your abilities and achievements. You will begin to live instead of just surviving. You will not have to pretend everything is okay. You will walk in love and practice forgiveness. You will not walk in resentfulness or bitterness.

Learn to enjoy the harmony in your life. When you are connected to the right people and things, you will impact your life and fuel others. Turn your vision into action so you can step outside your comfort zone, ready to take each step. Unleash the power within so you can filter all your life experiences through God's plan. We must believe we are loved, worthy, and accepted by Him. We are confident enough to go after unsuppressed dreams.

Women are not born confident. We must learn the specific steps and techniques to become confident not only as women but in our daily decision-making. "No" is a word we need to practice as we move forward. If we say yes to everything and everyone, we will be all over the place instead of the *right* place.

How do you know when you need to set boundaries? If you are experiencing an increased and sustained level of off-putting emotion, particularly resentment or anxiety, chances are you have identified a part of your life that lacks emotional, mental, or physical boundaries. Beware of internalizing others' moods and emotions too. Internalization can initially feel like empathy but may signify a lack of emotional boundaries.

Wisdom is the very thing we need to help our lives leave the cocoon stage and transform into butterflies. Wisdom will help every area of our life in which we want to grow and see fruit. We need wisdom in our relationships, careers, finances, faith, health, and overall life. Wisdom is always choosing to do what is right at all costs. The Bible reminds us there are more worthy pursuits than the search for treasure.

Proverbs 3:13-15

Blessed is the one who finds wisdom, and the one who gets understanding, for the gain from her is better than the form of silver and her profit better than gold. She is more precious than jewels, and nothing you desire can compare with her.

Wisdom and understanding are your personal treasure chest. We may think earthly riches will give us the good and easy life, but attached to wisdom is long life, pleasant ways, peaceful paths, and blessings. Wisdom gives us the ability to think and act, utilizing knowledge, understanding, experience, common sense, and insight.

The starting point in gaining wisdom is to fear God. Trust in the Lord with all your heart and rely not on your own understanding. In all your ways, acknowledge him, and he shall direct your path. When we obey God and live by holy principles, we will have better health and a longer, happier, and more prosperous life. Even when we are afflicted, and it seems like things are not looking up, we are to trust the Lord.

Trusting the Lord with our whole heart is the opposite of doubting God and His Word. God is trustworthy! It is easier to live on our own, but rest assured, we cannot afford to live outside of God's leading, His divine providence. We have to become uninterested in caring for ourselves. We must become uninterested in carrying others' burdens! We must adapt to the ways of God and adjust to the new condition. What is this "new condition"? Being good to you!

When you adapt and make adjustments, *being good to you* becomes possible. When you practice *being good to you*, your surroundings will respect you; your growth will demand it! *Being good to you* is a lifestyle, an everyday awareness that you must take care of yourself. This needs to be fully embraced; your mind needs to shift toward this change. You are crossing over when you no longer put yourself on the back burner! Ask yourself: "Who is really going to look after me or take care of me?" We are thankful for the people who would step up, but we must first step up for ourselves. We must speak up for ourselves and set boundaries that do not permit things meant to harm, hurt, or delay us. *Being good to you* is not seasonal; it is a committed and dedicated practice.

Being good to you means understanding your value and the worth of your existence! It is time to cross over and be good to you.

Chapter 7

BEING WOKE EVERY DAY

A tribute to women who once hid and lived in the shadows who are now revolutionized!

People hate rules at every stage of life, but they respect them because they produce order and good results. *Being good to You* has rules that must be maintained to live in that realm.

Three realms affect our ability to be good to ourselves. The first one is the realm of yesterday! Yesterday is a past tense word; it is not today or tomorrow and will never exist again. But ninety percent of our lives are directed or influenced by data from years of yesterdays. How many weekly conversations remind you of your yesterday pains, disappointments, and failures? We must not just recognize yesterday's data but release it to gain the strength and power to be good to us.

When we are deeply involved in yesterday, we drag it into our new day. We become so consumed by all the "yesterday stuff" that our new days become wasted, unproductive, and unprofitable. We wonder, "Where has this year gone?" Let's answer that! As the clock ticks on, we are consistently living in a realm that keeps us stuck! There is a proper way to handle the yesterday realm; we must keep it in proper alignment and have the right perspective. We must learn to exit each day with better care and forgive ourselves. When we ask the hard questions, we can learn from our failures or our mistakes. We need to realize that sometimes we live in ways that hinder our growth. When we do not confront those bad habits, we give yesterday permission to postpone our future.

When yesterday is gone, we must live in *the now*. The now is the second realm that must be lived with care so we can stop repeating bad cycles of yesterdays. The now is a strategic place that will keep you well-balanced and inspire major change. Why is the *now realm* important? This is a loaded question that needs our response. The *now realm* is present tense and inspires us to live with alertness, awareness, and sensitivity. When we are living in the now, we must handle time with care.

Living in the Spirit is how we must move so we can fulfill the third realm, the future. Living in the now, you must confront your fears of what was and what doesn't yet exist! We are afraid of so many things, like being unqualified, feeling inadequate, and being doubtful. We might ask questions like, "Why me?" or say, "I can't because of yesterday." God has given us a new frame to live in.

Hebrew 11:1

Now faith is the confidence in what we hope for and assurance about what we do not see.

When we have faith in the now, we believe in more than us. We believe in the unseen God and His heavenly resources bringing light to every part of our lives. We believe in the fruit of the Spirit.

Galatians 5:22-23

But the fruit of the Spirit is love, joy, peace, patience, kindness, goodness, faithfulness, gentleness, and self-control.

When we grow with each one of these fruits, we begin to live in the now, which teaches us to be good to us. Living in the now helps us become healthier, whole, and profitable beings.

I love knowing the Lord is my shepherd, and I shall not want or lack any good thing.

The third realm is the future! The future realm is waiting for our arrival, but we don't live in this realm until we've properly lived in the now. Not *being good to you* means something is off. Being aware of your life will create signals that will indicate you are off track. Being off the grid will lock you out of your future. Living in our yesterdays must come to a halt.

Matthew 6:34

So do not worry about tomorrow, for tomorrow will worry about itself. Each day has enough trouble of its own.

We must follow these rules to exit our yesterdays with care. How do we live in the future? We live in our future through the Spirit! Living through the Spirit enlightens us and gives us Godly wisdom to act and move in life. The Spirit is an open door that will help us live in our Future. The future realm is where we realize we have the advantage of a great future. This is promised in the following verse.

Jeremiah 29:11

"For I know the plans I have for you," declares the Lord, "plans to prosper you and not to harm you, plans to give you hope and a future."

How do we live in the advantaged place? Walking in healing! Healing is the children's bread. When we are walking in the provision of healing, understanding the price paid with the stripes of Jesus, we see the eternal position that established an advantage in our lives against the present realm. To walk in this advancement, we must learn to do maintenance on our emotions. We must become stable and fixed!

Did you know uncontrolled emotions create life burdens that will make you sick? Here's an example: when you are always sad and complain about everything, somewhere, you are disconnected; these things are depleting you. Healing is an inner, deep work that lifts the burdens of disappointments or heartaches! Healing helps you see the good in all things in life! Healing shows you a way of escape; it strengthens you to walk through the waters so you will not drown! Healing helps you operate in the now so you can enter your dreams and find your destiny. Jesus has given us a beautiful formula, which appears in the following verse.

Matthew 11:29

Take my yoke upon you. Let me teach you, because I am humble and gentle at heart, and you will find rest for your souls.

We can live beautifully in the now because we are not alone. We are learning from Jesus, the lover of our souls. When we take on His character and submit to His leadership, we will see our lives move and flow.

Where do we go from here? We deal with the uncircumcised heart, that addiction of mistreatment, the flooding of our souls confining our movement. We must stop living in the safety net that is our zone of comfort. Comfortable living means drinking from different wells; it will keep you running on a dead-end road.

It is time to face today! Coming face-to-face with the guts to own your beauty, your imperfections, but stepping with God, means becoming the *new you*. When you let God move in without limits, you will break out of your comfort zone.

You will disrupt the things that hindered your growth. When you begin to welcome the interruption, you will become the disrupter.

What is a disrupter? A simple but profound definition is a person who shakes things up. A disruptor brings change. A disruptor is an innovator. Disruption takes living through God because it is through Him that we are strong and mighty. This is why there is no room to live outside God's best intentions for your life. You were designed to fit His plans, not yours. Our plans conflict with His, saying, "Do not enter!" Our plans cause hiding, living under an open realm where anything comes and goes.

Being good to you is our goal; we get there through the doors of Christ. We must allow him to be the roof that covers us and the floor we stand on; He will give us all things according to His will. You must drink from His well! Allow Him to fill your cup until it overflows, and push take away yesterday's pains. Let Him help you navigate your now and prepare you to walk in your future. Living this way is the *revolution of women.*

The *revolutionized woman* is different from the normal. Her speech and responses to things are on a higher level. It's the opposite of what one will do and what one should do! Put down your natural weapons and pick up the weapons that will destroy inhibitors to your life.

Being a revolutionized woman means reflecting Kingdom principles. It means showing you're marked for Christ, letting His will shine on your path to draw your steps toward destiny. God's language, His ways, His plans have to be our new hunger and thirst. Do you want to revolutionize your life? Then submit to change no matter where you are! I know it's easier said than done, but when you do submit, He can and will transform impossibilities into possibilities.

Grab your walking shoes; let your feet be shod with the preparation of the Word of God. Grab your hat, your helmet of salvation. Every spiritual weapon is yours; use them.

Chapter 8

THE SPIRIT OF A CHAMPION

A tribute to women who awaken from the cave!

When you have lived in a cave, in the dark for so long, the things you carried for years begin to rule your life! It's time to step out of the cave and allow God's mighty waterfall to awaken you!

It is unreasonable to stay where you weren't designed to. Why? Because *the spirit of a champion* lives deep inside you. When I was in the bottomless pit of the cave, I counted myself out! I thought it was over. I thought I had lost it all. Until a small light entered my cave and called my name, saying, "Erica! Get. Up. From. There!" I responded with understanding; the light must be the spirit of a champion. There is a song I love, whose words are empowering.

This little light of mine,

I'm gonna let it shine.

Let it shine, let it shine, let it shine!

Before "This Little Light of Mine" became part of my testimony, I had to endure and persevere. The darkness that prevailed in my life became the ammunition I used to rise. All I needed was a glimpse of light, and I knew I was going to survive. The pain and the grime constantly trying to shape me only awoke the power of the spirit of a champion within me.

Reality stared me in the face, and the evidence was true. If I was not willing to live, no one else was going to do it for me. The grime embedded in my life wasn't pretty. I was like clay in other people's hands; I was being molded by life and how others viewed it. I had to remind myself constantly until it became my anthem: if you don't live, no one else is going to do it for you.

The clock continued to tick. For the majority of my days and nights, I was lost, confused, and broken by the grime. Suicidal thoughts were always on my mind. The heaviness in my life produced a pouring rain that left me sad for years. I reached out for help; I turned to people I thought had the light. They weren't ready for a girl like me. Their judgements, their criticism made a bed of mud for me to stay trapped in.

When I looked to my left, and to my right, I was surrounded by clouds of darkness, hovering over me, producing negativity. I lived in the negative. The grime I had allowed to be the boss of me finally pushed me to a place I thought I would never see. There, in the bottomless pit, I heard a man's voice saying, "Get up from there!" I was Lazarus, wrapped from head to toe in grave clothes. Every torn piece of fabric wrapped around me screamed: she has no purpose, no dreams, no hope. The garments of fear squeezed the very life out of me and filled my days with the aroma of death.

I came to understand there is only one way out, and His name was Jesus. I called on Jesus. This was not easy for me because shame had swallowed me whole. The first step in seeing beauty in the ashes was that I had to believe. Believe I could rise, that I could become more. Believe I could do more— that I could have more. When I believed, the light came on, and I realized my life was not over. My life matters, and others' opinions are just that: opinions.

I consistently believed and agreed with a substance greater than those circumstances that led to my regression. Choosing to believe in truth changed the order of my life; it set me free! Freedom was necessary for me so I could live.

Freedom gave me a surpassing strength and confidence that breathed hope back into my dry bones. Freedom rebuilt the walls keeping out anything that would compromise my destiny. If one doesn't believe, one will never get started on their destiny. My belief became stronger, and my outlook sharpened. I had to allow God to change my atmosphere because where I was standing could not tolerate my growth. That environment was not good soil; it could not cultivate my life. It was time to let go of my familiar surroundings so I could arrive at God's appointed place.

What I visualized for my life was not yet in focus! I still had bad habits creating patterns that wanted me to believe this was as far as I could go. I learned quickly that focusing on the negative was a prison cell that would never release me. By removing myself from the toxic environment, I had to count the cost. I had to understand in each season there are choices, oppositions, requirements, preparations, disciplines, separations, growths, and rewards.

In my next phase of life, I knew it was not going to be easy, but I finally understood what I desired.

Luke 18:27

What is impossible with man is possible with God.

What I desired was to please the one who holds my life in His hands. I desired to finish my life strong. Will I get knocked down? Sure. But the beauty is in the getting up. Champions understand the balance of life.

Philippians 4:11-13

For I have learned in whatever situation I am to be content. I know how to be brought low, and I know how to abound. In any and every circumstance, I have learned the secret of facing plenty and hunger, abundance and need. I can do all things through Him who strengthens me.

Balance is not something given; it is a process of building, letting go, trusting, being honest and disciplined, and having plenty of patience. My past failures, experiences, discouragements, setbacks, and high expectations were a combination of scars, my *champion marks*, that allowed me to spread hope. Living used to be a challenge, and my life was based on those of everyone else. Now, with my eyes wide open, I see the beauty of what this life is and *my* place in it. I no longer live beneath the grime, the negativity. I live above, soaring high, like an eagle spreading my wings of freedom.

One early morning, I went through a drastic life event that pushed me outside of myself. I was so depressed; I ate six hamburgers in one sitting. I ran into the bathroom and vomited so badly that the hamburger came through my nose. I cried and cried; poetry began to arise. I grabbed my journal, my favorite pen, and began to write the lines to release the negativity within.

POLISHING MY JEWELS HIDDEN IN MY BACKYARD

Shhh. Listen! Do you hear it? Can you see it? Come closer; it's within your view.

The sound of the shovel digging for something rare.

In my days of darkness, a beam of hope wants to reveal itself.

The voices of many labels saying, "Not you, not now!"

You are not the right shade nor the right size.

Shhh. Listen as the shovel increases its pressure.

The weight of it declares silence from you.

But oh! By my surprise, what I thought was my demise, I realize I was optimized and mobilized to come alive.

Every swing from the shovel was a layer of defeat, which added a layer of discouragement, which became the process of the death of me.

I was found underneath the grime; I couldn't see but that was the place I needed to be. The rain began to pour and pour; I was still there, but nobody could hear my voice.

I knew all along I had a song, but I was buried beneath the opinions, what others consider right or wrong.

Shhh. Listen, do you hear the footsteps that are near?

They still don't realize I have always been here. The work of the shovel

begins again; they are still looking for something rare. By

that time, the rain had released me from the mind of disguised.

Shhh. Listen. Yes, that is me, living boldly before all eyes to see.

Living in such a way that life becomes a melody.

My walk and my talk become different, and my look is spot on.

I didn't need to be found by no one.

I only had to believe to become.

As time passes and dreams are lived, no introduction will be needed because it will be shining so deep that it inspires hearts to beat.

The shovel will always be there, but I realize the rain will come; it will pour and it will water me from head to toe. To awaken the gifts for more.

Shhh. Listen, it's the sound of my heart shouting, "Yes, it's me!"

It's my time to release.

These lyrics woke me from my cave and brought a smile to my face. At that moment, I stood in strength and decided it was time to be brave.

I was released from the voice of pain; there, the exchange was made.

The spirit of a champion began to reign. You must only revisit the cave when you are in control. The cave is the place you make decisions, but you should never make it your home. Now that you are out of the cave, make it known you are *alive* and *well*!

Chapter 9

RESCUE HER

A tribute to those who wanted to jump off the cliff because that seemed like the only option. Suicide is real, but Jesus is greater!

A small voice whispered to me, "Kill her!" So, I hit myself in the face with my own bare hands, punishing myself, reflecting on the negativity and abuse in my life. "You are worthless!" Worthless means having no real value or substance! I felt useless and ashamed; a deep cry within begged me to die! I did not love me, although I wanted to. I wanted love so bad I thought his fist was his way of showing his love to me.

One day, after cleaning up my house (not my home), I walked to the laundromat with my and my son's clothes. As I was going to the change machine to get quarters, a man walked up and spoke to me. As innocent as this interaction was, my supposed boyfriend got angry. He hit me with his knuckles, right on the temple above my eye, as my son watched. The licks I received—for anything from "Take off that red lipstick, now!" to checking if I was wearing any underwear! I will never forget how he put a winter hat on my head and pulled it over my eyes because he wanted no one to see me—not even myself! I spent two years being afflicted and living in a broken place.

Erica was silenced! I was raped by him over and over again! I was in a spiritual coma. Darkness lived in me and controlled my life. The sad thing? We both went to church. He was wicked; his plot was to kill every dream within me!

The only reason he went to church was to control who I talked to, to make sure I did not ask for help. The church I was attending sent the church van to pick us up! I would pray to God to *get me out of this.* I wanted out! I did not need a Bible story, because I was headed to death.

Believe it or not, the house I was living in was condemned. The landlord refused to replace the old wires because all he wanted was the rent—which I could barely pay. When the house caught on fire, I thought, *God, if I can find a house close to church, I will walk to church every day!* Now that I look back at that unlivable, burned-up house, I realize God was delivering me from bondage! He was offering me a new life, and I was ready for it!

The little blue house I found is where he gave me his last beating, negative words, and hands around my neck. I just knew my life was over! He was asleep on the couch, and my son was asleep in the bedroom. I grabbed the Clorox, went to the bathroom, sat on the floor, and untwisted the cap. I lifted the Clorox to drink the last drink of my life. I was about to kiss death! The whisper said, "Kill her!" But then I saw the shadow of my son's footsteps. As he walked toward me from the bedroom, I heard him say, "Mom, who is going to take care of me?" Tears ran down my face as I cried ferociously.

A supernatural strength came over me, telling me to ask for help! "Help me" were the words I needed to tell the right person. When I went back to church that Sunday, I was looking for a sermon. I was looking for someone to help me, to rescue me! God allowed it. I moved some furniture into her home, and there I was, detangling from my mess. I had a desire to move closer to him, but I was in need of something greater than that man could offer me!

Let me explain: this woman embraced me and my son. She rescued me. But tell me, despite that rescue, why I was planning to move back with him. After a day of scheming to get a new place, at midnight, I packed everything in his car. I believed he was going to change, that we were headed somewhere special in life. I was watching too many love stories on television. What happened next took me for a ride!

We arrived at the house, located on a dead-end road, and unloaded the car. I was the last person to enter. The door shut and, immediately, God said, I am going to deliver you! Tears ran down my face; I knew what was about to happen. His Presence was in the house. That night, as I lay prostrate on the living room floor, I prayed to the Holy Spirit. I prayed for hours, and then He spoke again, "You were rescued naturally. Man would have received credit for your transformation, but I am about to set you free!"

The process was grueling. My boyfriend became so hostile that I could not even kick him out of the house. I had to evict him! I did not want to, but I was at a dead-end in my life. I had to turn around and walk through this—not run from it. I had to face this man face-to-face and know God was with me! Ten days is what the magistrate gave him before he had to leave. Then, my restraining order would go into full effect. Do you know this man hid my phone and would not allow me or my son to leave my house?

Everything I told you before—he did it all over again. The rape, the abuse—it was worse! After ten days were up, he went to sleep after keeping a tight leash on me. I couldn't even use the bathroom by myself. I sent my young son to knock on my neighbor's door and call 911. My boyfriend did not realize my son had left to get help. I stayed peaceful and loving toward him, even though I hated him. When the police pulled up, he ran out the door. I knew I received what only God can give! I could have listened to that voice and killed myself and that was the hidden agenda, I had an illegal death warrant, but God knew it was not the end. People love to say God does not hear a sinner's prayer, but not only did he hear my prayer he came for the sick and not the well. I was in need of a Savior! It was time to make the committed move from the kingdom of darkness to the Kingdom of light.

I was my own worst enemy. Why? I loved others before I loved myself and put everyone's interests above my own. This is how I went wrong on so many levels. What I learned as I made transitions: there is an order to my life. It is not selfish to love yourself first! We must know this order so we can function well. We need to listen well, so we don't stay broken people with broken hearts and broken lives.

What is the order for living and thriving? First, love the Lord your God with all your heart, might, and strength. Second, love your neighbor as you love yourself. Everything else comes after this order. When you are committed to God and committed to loving yourself, your life moves properly. You're guaranteed to reach greater heights of real love and healthy relationships. We cannot love people or build upon healthy relationships outside of this order.

Chapter 10

BEING GOOD TO ME IS MY NEW PURPOSE

A tribute to every woman who understands her worth!

I choose me! I have to choose me, you have to choose you, if we are going to live out God's promises in our lives. The journey is hard when you leave God out of the picture and allow people and things only there for your downfall. It is easier when you have chosen Jesus Christ as your Lord and Savior because His ways are easier. Come close to God; taste and see that God is good.

As I was walking through the lowest valleys of my life, I remember people saying, "God is good," but I didn't know that truth for myself. I began to wonder, what does good really mean if I'm only experiencing heartache and pain? If He is good, why doesn't He send some goodness my way? I was bitter, full of anger, and suicidal. I was weak and hopeless; my soul was afflicted. I asked myself, what is wrong with me? What makes our lives broken?

I knew it was time to turn my life around. The odds in life are stronger because we have been in a stuck position. But we must try. Right? I used to love playing vinyl records. Today, that smooth sound is hard to find. When the song starts skipping, it is hard to let it play out! Especially when it is repeating itself over and over again! It's time to ask myself, "Am I going to continue to listen to a broken record? Or change the record to a new one?" It's time to get a new one! We have already cleaned the record with alcohol, and nothing changed. So yes, it's time for a change!

Every day is a chance to choose to *be good to you*. No longer will I accept men putting their hands on me without any consequences. No longer will I let people remain in my life who are negative or of unequal yoke. No longer will I accept disrespect from anyone intentionally trying to hurt me.

When we, as women, act immature about who we are, the enemy strikes. The enemy of our soul does not care how he afflicts us. He holds back nothing if we don't stand our ground. What is immature? Being immature is lacking wisdom, insight, and emotional stability. We must become mature. Being mature means reaching full development and balance; mentally, emotionally, and spiritually. It means doing the work to keep our peace and not allowing unhealthy habits to overrun our true identity. We must move differently if we are going to become mature women.

We have to become women who know how to create boundaries and stand their ground! How do we create a boundary? Mark the place of your peace, your new direction, and draw a line that says: these are my limits. Nothing can penetrate that sphere unless you remove the boundary. Removing the boundary should not be an option. We must remember why we created it in the first place. We created the boundary so we can see maturity in all areas of our lives.

We must take our stand! How do we take our stand? We must be willing to *be good to us*! We must care about every inch of our lives and keep them at a healthy level. We must stand and stop being people-pleasers. We must intentionally change the pattern of being a pushover. We must be deliberate about our assertiveness. Being assertive speaks volumes to how much you value your worth; it demands people take you more seriously. When you stand up for yourself, you obtain essential self-confidence to help you confront your issues with others and look out for your well-being.

Beauty from ashes is a mark on those women who have gone through the fire and come out with the sound of freedom in their lives. The fire did not kill me; it made me. The ashes represent a loss. Looking at all the ashes in my life, I knew I must be a woman who would rise from the ashes. The opposite of ashes is beauty. Beauty is what I needed in my life. Not vain beauty but a crown of beauty.

Did you know beauty is a crown? The crown of beauty, rising from the ashes, evokes a sense of comeback, of a phoenix rising from destruction, of finding something good amid so much evil.

Isaiah 14:24

Surely as God has planned, so it will be, and as He has purposed, so it will happen.

You will emerge from the ashes as a new phoenix. You will be fully restored. You will be re-established. You will roar. Today, I stand, having access to the promise I saw in my vision and heard from the heart of God. I am not finished yet, but I am on the right path! I am no longer fighting with flesh and trying to be. I am no longer that girl; I am a woman now! I did not know the strength I carried. I said, "I did not know how much strength I carried!" Now that I am in a better place in my life, as I look at my old self, whose eyes were full of darkness because…Pause. See, it's easier to say, "because" and name off the list of painful things that drove your life into despair. Unpause! I now see I allowed these things to take place. I know it's hard to accept that we don't take care of the one person we are truly responsible for ourselves!

Me! I am responsible for me. I let others rule her, beat her, speak down to her, and embarrass her. I allowed things in my life that depleted me. I felt invaluable and worthless. The sad thing is, the root cause of these feelings was poor self-treatment. I didn't know how to *be good to me*. I was alive, but unconscious and uncertain. I was living in a daze, locked in a maze, destroying my life without realizing how much danger I was consistently battling. I was in a daydream about my life situations. What is daydreaming? Daydreaming is the stream of consciousness that detaches from current, external tasks when attention drifts to a more personal and internal direction. I was living inside a bubble; I wanted it popped to alleviate the pain. I needed oxygen. Not just oxygen for my lungs but spiritual oxygen for my soul.

How does a person move out of a defeated life? This question was the first of many I had to ask to see the need for change. We can't change if we don't see the change we need to make. It was time to grab opportunities that were all around me, but that dead place kept me in the dark! I needed the light to turn on in my life so I could stop going through broken cycles. I needed a deeper touch, one that man can never quench.

I was like the woman at the well, hiding. She purposely showed up to the well early, to beat the crowd. She had many secrets and lived in dark places. Just like other women, she wanted to change, but how could she change when her life was a mess? Perhaps she said what we say today, "Why even try?" That was no longer my confession; I was going to try.

I have hope now. I have a desire in my spirit for change. Deep down is a desire to be good to ourselves and follow God. Jesus was at the well; he knew what the woman needed. He asked for a drink, then flipped it on her, saying, "If you knew who asked you for a drink, you would have asked me for a drink." What he was offering her was a cup of salvation, deliverance, and Himself. This is what God was telling me, and now telling you: "Drink from me and you will never thirst again."

It is time to access your *promotion*! It is time to get to the "sweet spot of life" that is your destiny. Promotion is another step closer to God. When God promotes you, you are another step closer to His best intentions for your life. How do you access the promotion?

James 4:10

Humble yourselves before the Lord and He will promote you.

In a believer's life, understand all promotion is accomplished by God and God alone. No longer shall we get caught in the wind of looking for man to promote and reward us. They can't! Promotion does not come from the east, south, or west; it comes from the Lord. If we want man's promotion, we will always be indebted to man. We will owe them, and God doesn't want us to owe any man anything but love.

Yes, scream! In fact—roar! God has rewarded you with His grace and mercy, renewed each morning! When we stoop down low to see God, He, in turn, is exalted, and brings our lives to completion. This is the season to increase in God and decrease in self so our true lives will be found. God doesn't make our lives easier; He makes life better, makes us stronger. God's promotion is not connected to your position; it's connected to His Presence. Promotion that comes from God comes from His increased Presence in your life. The Presence of God is God's promotion. When He is at the center of our lives, God gives us His power and the awareness of His Glory. In return, we must understand favor follows faithfulness, and favor leads to fruitfulness. It is time to take a position of power, first in the land of our lives, then flowing into the place he calls us to walk. May we rise with the torch in our hands, roaring, "Come out!" and saying, "This is the way!" God has not brought us this way for nothing. He has brought us here for such a time as this! This is the moment we will walk differently and mature in God. This is the moment we will learn the weapon of *being good to me* is where the oil will flow. Arise, daughters of the highest God, and learn to *be good to you*! Roar!

ABOUT THE AUTHOR

Erica Jett is a devoted wife, a loving mother, and a joyful grandmother. She is also the CEO and Founder of The Empowerment Palace Firm, where she releases her potential at maximum strength, bringing effective change to individuals, families, ministries, and communities.

As a certified Christian counselor, Erica Jett is a change agent for men and women from all walks of life, teaching them to crack the code of the many emotional diseases they face on a daily basis.

She is a leader who shapes and sharpens teens through her course, "Teens Exiting Program." Erica is an encourager to many young children in her Kids Character Club. She raises their self-esteem and self-awareness, building their core of being exceptionally strong leaders who are the future.

Erica Jett is also an ordained Pastor and Leader of The Gospel who studied Christian ministry at More than Conquerors College in Charlotte, NC. She partners with several ministers to build spiritual bridges for people to cross over.

Erica's servanthood and leadership skills are well known in surrounding cities and states as the she travels, pouring real empowerment, real conversation, as people experience real change.

Erica Jett is The President of Females Speaking Up, where she empowers with high motivation and encouragement. She has released her first book, *Be Good to You!*, which will be an anthem to women everywhere! Erica Jett is also the podcast host of The Empowerment Palace Morning Show on Spotify.

She is an inspirational voice for abusive women by sharing her life story that inspired her to write and produce the drama titled *The Voices of Rescued Women.*

www.ingramcontent.com/pod-product-compliance
Lightning Source LLC
Chambersburg PA
CBHW051553120626
46551CB00013B/1493